A nostalgic look at

EDINBURGH TRAMS

Since 1950

A NOSTALGIC LOOK AT EDINBURGH TRAMS SINCE 1950

CONTENTS

AUTHOR'S ACKNOWLEDGEMENTS

THE writing of any book, especially with a historic theme, always involves a number of people who have helped and advised in all sorts of ways. This publication is no exception and those not mentioned specifically in the following paragraphs may be assured of my grateful thanks.

There are, however, one or two particular people who do deserve a special mention. Top of the list is Neil Mackenzie, the General Manager and Executive Director of Lothian Region Transport, whose enthusiasm has been a great source of both inspiration and assistance in making progress with this book. Many of the photographs featured in these pages are from LRT's archives and are credited.

I am also deeply indebted to Michael Ashworth, of the Scottish Mining Museum. His tireless efforts in helping compile captions, through extensive research into historical archives, have been magnificent. Without his assistance, the book would have taken much longer to produce.

As with my previous book about Glasgow trams, due credit should go to John Fozard, of Baildon, West Yorkshire, for his superb printing of some of the historic negatives. Thanks also to the other photographic contributors, who produced some marvellous material.

My thanks also to Martin Jenkins, for his introduction to Hannah Gordon, who has written a most charming and evocative Foreword.

Finally, I would like to thank my wife Kendal, and sons Matthew and Alastair, who have, on many occasions, had to 'take a back seat' whilst I was occupied in research and writing.

Graham Twidale, Blackpool, Lancashire, September 1989.

Copyright © Graham Twidale &
Silver Link Publishing Ltd.

Designed by Barbara Allen/
Leading Edge Press & Publishing.

Jacket design by Nigel Harris.

First published in the United
Kingdom, October 1989.

Twidale, Graham
    A nostalgic look at edinburgh trams since
1950.
    1. Scotland. Trams, history
I. Title
625'.6609411

Imagesetting by Ps&Qs, Liverpool and printed in the United Kingdom by The Amadeus Press, Huddersfield, Yorkshire.

FRONT COVER: A classic view of one of Edinburgh's madder-and-white tramcars (No. 204) turning out of Hanover Street in 1956. *D.G. Clark.*

REAR COVER: Standard car No. 214 at the east end of Princes Street, in 1954. *David Packer Collection.*

THIS PAGE: This was probably Edinburgh's busiest tramway junction, at the eastern end of Princes Street. In Waterloo Place today (the street running to the right of *The Waterloo)* can be seen Edinburgh's memorial to its trams; a short section of cable track has been relaid in the middle of the road. Domed-roof Standard cars Nos. 217 (left) and 40 are shown passing each other on Services 11 and 14 respectively. Car 217 was the last car to enter Shrubhill, on the final night of operations on November 16 1956. The lady crossing the road on the right typifies the high fashion of the period - 1955. The tracks in Waterloo Place had gone by this time. *David Packer Collection.*

FOREWORD
by
HANNAH GORDON

I am very fond of trams. A smile can come to my lips when, in conversation, someone perhaps says: "....we used to take a tram from the square and go to....." An old photograph which shows a tram will set me thinking of my early days in Edinburgh. "....oh, that's the corner where the chemist was.....still is..... but the trams alas, no more."

All this shows that I must have a very forgiving nature, for at approximately the age of four years, I was nearly obliterated by one of Edinburgh's tramcars. It happened outside the Peacock Hotel in the then-thriving fishing port of Newhaven, in Edinburgh. I was out shopping with my mother, as usual pushing my doll's pram which was furnished, not with the customary doll, but (for some never-explained reason) with a long-suffering car who would put up with being dressed in a bonnet and wheeled around Edinburgh!

On this particular day, my mother paused to talk to a friend in the main street. I spotted a friend of my own on the opposite side of the road. Looking to neither left or right, I belted across - the poor tramcar never stood a chance! I remember 'coming to' some time later in my granny's bed, presumably not too much the worse for wear. My elder brother's conviction that this explains why I am 'soft in the heid' to this day is probably not too far from the truth! The same brother, Richard, retains a passionate interest in Edinburgh's trams, and one of his photographs of a works car appears on page 58. His impression of the noise a tramcar made as it progressed along Princes Street is still revered in certain quarters!

One had the same affection for a tramcar as a steam train; a tramcar had identity - a personality of its own. You were *fond* of a tramcar - although, if you ever found yourself between a pair of them, travelling in opposite directions, whilst crossing the road, you never lost your respect for them, even after my earlier experience.

A regular Sunday outing with my Great Aunt Maggie would include a ride on a tram from Newhaven, to, say, the terminus at Fairmilehead. We'd sit there a few minutes whilst the tram driver had a rest and a chat, before he walked the length of the car to drive it from the other end, all the way back to Newhaven.

On the trams, the conductors and conductresses were your friends. Sometimes you would meet one of them 'off-duty' and remark how different they looked in civvies. The men always looked younger in their uniforms, and the conductresses always found a variety of ingenious ways to wear their caps to accommodate their hair styles. They always seemed to be great 'characters' and I recall the glee I experienced one Christmas morning unwrapping a toy 'conductors set.'

This book will delight all tram enthusiasts and bring back happy memories for those of us who were just enthusiastic passengers.

Hannah Gordon.

A NOSTALGIC LOOK AT EDINBURGH TRAMS SINCE 1950

INTRODUCTION

THE enormous success of my earlier book *A Nostalgic Look at Glasgow Trams since 1950* persuaded Silver Link Publishing and myself to venture into print again, this time featuring the trams which once graced the streets of Edinburgh. However, it is important to stress from the start, as with the Glasgow book, that this is not intended to be either a definitive history, nor is it designed solely for the tramway enthusiast. Others, far better qualified than I, have covered these aspects expertly and professionally. Hopefully, this book will give pleasure not only to those interested in trams for their own sake,

but also to those who simply used to live and work in Edinburgh, and recall the days when the streets echoed to the hum of electric motors and the squeal of wheel flanges. The greater number of the photographs in these pages recall the city and its trams since 1950, but a few views do pre-date this particular year, to set the scene and provide background interest.

Compared with its great rival, Glasgow, the Edinburgh tramway system was smaller, though throughout its history, probably far more complex in historical terms. Methods of traction ranged from the horse, an

experiment with steam, cable and, finally, electric traction. And this was just in Edinburgh itself – the story becomes more complex yet when Musselburgh and Leith are taken into consideration! An outline history is provided on pages 9-17.

The system began work in 1871 and ran in its various guises until a rousing send-off saw the final procession of cars leave Braids and head for Shrubhill for the last time on Friday November 16 1956. This seemingly nonsensical withdrawal of a proven electric public transport system, in favour of the diesel bus, proceeded despite the Suez crisis and

Above: The epitome of 'modern' Edinburgh tramcars: domed-roof Standard No. 172 poses in the Meadows, fresh from the paint-shop, in 1950. The clean lines and perfect proportions of the car are shown to good effect. No. 172 survived until the end of the tramway system, only six years away, eventually as a decorated car, in the last days of tram working. *LRT.*

impending fuel shortages which meant rationing for all vehicles!

In terms of passengers carried each year, the 12-months period ending in May 1947 holds the record with a staggering total of 192,892,899. In the same year, the buses also carried 83,487,790 people. The current Lothian Regional Transport organisation would dearly love to have those sort of figures today!

Although it is now almost 33 years since the last cars ran on Services 23 and 28, from Morningside Station to Granton Road Station and Braids to Stanley Road, a glance through these pages will, hopefully, revive happy memories for many people, both those still resident in Edinburgh and those exiled in far-flung outposts of the world.

Again, unlike Glasgow, Edinburgh has, in comparative terms, changed very little in appearance; no motorways have ravaged the city centre and many fine buildings remain in situ. Development has been considerate and controlled. Most buildings of course, have now been cleansed of the decades of soot and grime which filled the atmosphere until a few years ago – and gave the city its *Auld Reekie* nickname. One of the last of the blackened monoliths, the North British Hotel, was being cleaned and renovated as this book went to press, but there were no signs of an attempt to 'brush up' the Scott monument.

Princes Street, some might say, has never been the same since the trams disappeared. There always seemed to be a constant procession of cars, majestically cruising back and forth, in their splendid livery of madder and white. They seemed to blend with their surroundings so well – and they were always immaculately clean, except perhaps on filthy, 'slushy' winter days. Before any withdrawals there were no less than 16 services using all or part of Princes Street.

1956, and the 1950s generally, had yet to witness the 'wind of change' which later became the trademark of the 'swinging sixties' and all that went with it. Modernisation and change for its own sake seemed to be the most common philosophy - but there was always the mini skirt! In the 1950s however, this was all in the future, and with the war fading into

Above: Granton Square, with the Harbour in the background, in 1954. Some harbour infill has taken place over the subsequent years with industrial units and stores being built on the reclaimed land. The Square was hitherto the terminus for no fewer than seven services. They were Nos: 2, 8, 9, 13,14,16, and 17. Here we see cars Nos. 195 and 107 meeting before returning to Colinton and Newington Station. The Square itself has changed little in character since this photograph was taken. The steam crane on the right appears to be giving cause for concern; close examination reveals that it has become derailed! *LRT.*

Above: The same scene on Tuesday September 12 1989. The trams are long gone and the railway is a memory too, recalled today only by the occasional piece of half-buried track on the roadside. There is now no commercial traffic into Granton's once-busy docks, which are now used as a marina, for leisure purposes. That being said, the atmosphere in the square is much the same, and public transport links into the city centre are maintained by Lothian Region Transport's buses, which still sport the historic madder-and-white livery once carried by the tramcars. *Nigel Harris.*

Left: From time to time, Edinburgh used its trams for decorating and advertising purposes. This practice started at Christmas/New Year 1933 and was to continue on an occasional basis until the end of tram working in 1956. Pictured here is wooden-bodied Standard car No. 58, used in October 1934 to promote Post Office Telephones, during a special 'telephone week' at that time. *LRT.*

history, all was apparently as it had been for decades. A post-war housing boom was under way, however, with new estates and schemes starting to spring up. Even so, this was still the age of the horse-drawn milk float and gas lamps still cast their warm yellow glow in side streets at night. In the early 1950s, thousands of Edinburgh people still used the trams either for work or pleasure trips to the zoo, the beach at Portobello or the races at Musselburgh.

At this time, the St. James Centre was still a planner's dream (or nightmare!), Princes Street shops looked much the same as they always had and Princes Street station (at the west end) was still a busy railway terminus. It too, is now history.

Study the photographs shown carefully. Notice the shops which have come and gone. Look at the advertisements on the trams and the street hoardings. Although many of the scenes have changed little over the years, two features are noticeably different today. The motor cars shown are, for the most part, now collectors items. For example, in 1956 there was a good three years to go before the advent of the enormously successful *Mini-Minor.* On the streets could be seen plenty of Morris Minors, Austins and Jowetts to name but three fondly-remembered cars.

Fashion, of course, is the other aspect of life which has changed drastically. A crowd of people generally looked fairly drab in those days, with the ubiquitous gaberdene mackintosh and rather muted colours of ladies dresses and coats. Compare these with the much brighter styles of today! Tram crews, of course, always seemed to be smartly turned-out, with their full uniforms, including the familiar peaked cap. These took on a slightly nautical flavour in the spring and summer periods when a white stretch-top was fitted, making them look particularly smart and eye-catching. Many photographs in the book show this feature.

The trams themselves also took on something of a festive air during royal visits, other special occasions and during the Festival. Three pennants of different colours or 'flags of all nations' were attached to their trolley ropes, providing an attractive splash of colour. One important feature of the cars themselves was the draught-excluding doors fitted on the platforms, to protect the driver's back during windy weather – which seems to occur in Edinburgh with regular frequency. This simple but effective device was much appreciated by motormen.

From 1953, and until some time after the final services had been

withdrawn, the streets in the city which had carried the trams were under the seemingly constant chaos of rebuilding, as the tramway was systematically erased from the cityscape. Rails were generally lifted soon after a route closed and the granite setts in which the rails had been laid were, for the most part, replaced by a tarmac surface. The sound of the pneumatic drill became an all-too-familiar part of city life – and, of course, it seems to have been so ever since! Traffic congestion as a result of this rebuilding caused havoc and gave many drivers a headache. One particular exception to the replacing of setts by tarmac was in Frederick Street; this was part of route 24, Waverley to Comely Bank, the first route to close, in 1952. Once the rails were lifted, the setts were replaced and exactly where the trams ran can be seen quite clearly to this day. One other location where a similar relaying took place was in Newhaven Main Street.

Edinburgh was to be the second of the four large Scottish city tram systems to be abandoned. Dundee was the first, a few weeks before Edinburgh, on October 20 1956. Aberdeen's trams followed the capital's cars into history on May 3 1958 and, of course, Glasgow ended it all on September 1 1962. I clearly remember the trams in Edinburgh in their final weeks, during a visit to the city on a school holiday in August 1956.

The thrill of riding up and down Princes Street and grinding up the Mound are treasured memories which in some ways now seem very distant, and yet which in other ways seem amazingly fresh.

Unlike the previous book, the photographs in the current publication are from various sources and have been duly acknowledged. Many have never been published before. Some are from the late Bob Mack's collection, now the property of David Packer and John Fozard. George Staddon produced these particularly fine views. The book is again divided into six principal chapters, with views from various parts of the city as well as one or two work-shop pictures and a handful of historic scenes. To highlight the degree of change, or in some cases the almost complete lack of it, I have included some 'past and present' comparative views. This provides a fascinating comparison of the degree of change witnessed over the last 30 or so years. It is all pure nostalgia. From timeless Marchmont and Morningside to the hurly-burly of the modern day city, the scenes contained in the book should, hopefully, evoke fond memories of a bygone age.

Picture Princes Street with its seemingly endless procession of trams (much the same as today's buses!). Remember the sound of the four wheel cars clattering over the many junctions, particularly the Post Office, Tollcross or the foot of Leith Walk; the protesting squeal of flanges as a Service 23 car negotiated the 'S' bend from the Mound, over Princes Street and up Hanover Street. In the latter years, when the trackwork was not all that it might have been, a certain amount of lurching, particularly if you were on the top deck, was noticeable to say the least! It all added, as one might say, to the character and appeal of the trams! There is much to see in the book to remind the reader of less-hurried times, to jog the memory about things that have been, and maybe even bring to mind people remembered from a generation ago.

Graham Twidale,
Blackpool,
Lancashire,
September 1989

Above: A familiar sight in the city during the last week of tram operation in November 1956. Domed-roof Standard car No. 172 was specially decorated for the occasion and toured the remaining lines to remind citizens that an aspect of life taken for granted for so long was about to disappear. Here we see Driver William Moffatt posing in front of No. 172 at Shrubhill. Despite its immaculate appearance and with only six years of service, No.172 was scrapped following abandonment. *LRT.*

A BRIEF HISTORY OF EDINBURGH'S TRAMWAYS

Above: A building of great historical significance – the power station and cable car depot at Henderson Row. This was constructed by the Edinburgh Northern Tramways Company in 1887, to power its cable routes, firstly to Goldenacre and subsequently Stockbridge. A 'gripper' on the cars was clamped onto a moving cable, in a conduit between the rails, to provide traction. The first route, from Hanover Street to Goldenacre, opened on January 28 1888. Almost 33 years to the day later, on January 24 1921, the power station closed. It was subsequently used as a bus depot and then as Edinburgh's police garage. It survived in virtually its original form – complete with sections of cable track – until early 1989, when it was largely demolished. Fortunately, the facade has been retained as part of the redevelopment, as a reminder of the early pioneering days of the cable tramway system. *LRT.*

THE word 'brief' must, in the context of this book, be taken quite literally, for the history of the tramways is indeed detailed and diverse. The complications between the City of Edinburgh, the Burghs of Leith and Musselburgh, not to mention the different traction systems used (horse, cable, steam and electricity) are many and varied. All this has been written about in greater detail by others far more competent in this field than myself, and those wishing to delve deeper into the finer detail of the Scottish capital's tram story would be well advised to visit their local libraries and borrow a copy of David L.G. Hunter's book, *Edinburgh's Transport* which is a phenomenally detailed publication and from which I have been able to glean a great deal of knowledge. I am indebted to him for permission to utilise information and quote passages. For our pur-

poses, a 'thumbnail' historical sketch will suffice, to set the scene.

The Edinburgh Tramways Act of 1871 authorised the Edinburgh Street Tramways Company to construct various tramway routes within Edinburgh, Leith and Portobello 'to be worked by animal power only' in other words horse-power! Thus began the tramway story which was to continue, in various forms, for the next 85 years.

The capital for this first company was £300,000 and construction had to

be completed within three years. The fares were generally not to exceed 1d per mile, the gauge was to be the standard railway gauge of four feet eight and a half inches – Sunday services were not intended. The horses pulling the cars had bells fitted to their harnesses and drivers were equipped with whistles to warn other traffic and passers-by of their approach.

The first service from Bernard Street to Haymarket was opened on Monday November 16 1871, without ceremony. Various other routes were opened over the following months. All, however, did not go smoothly. There were many complaints ranging from unguarded wheels (thought to be highly dangerous), parts of roadways were said to be too narrow, rail levels were claimed to be too high, horses were allegedly overworked and there were the inevitable accidents – some fatal, sadly.

Further acts of Parliament were passed over the next few years; these enabled the expansion of the system and also experimental use of a steam tram on the Portobello line. The second phase of tramway history duly came into being on April 23 1881, when a Kitson steam engine, hauling a passenger car, left Waterloo Place for Portobello.

A further engine subsequently joined the route, but this form of transport proved only moderately successful, for there were complaints about noise and smoke. Also, steam trams, according to those opposed to change, were not really 'the sort of thing' that Edinburgh should be involved with! They were not successful in any case, and the last example ran on October 27 1882.

Edinburgh Corporation acquired (by compulsory powers) that part of the system within its own boundaries from the company in 1892. Leith did not care for Edinburgh's high-handed attitude and these routes, together with those in Portobello, were operated by the company, as in the past. This division with Leith led to many years of separate tramway running, leading to much inconvenience to the travelling public, who had to switch from one organisation's cars to the other, at the relevant boundaries.

Meanwhile, a completely new system of tramway travel had been considered. The very nature of Edinburgh's hilly terrain made it difficult to run public transport of any sort. The horse trams never ventured down the steep hills to the north of the city – this had been left to the smaller horse buses. Furthermore, in bad weather as many as five horses had to be used to haul the vehicles; in ice and snow they didn't run at all. Clearly something had to be done. In San Francisco, a new form of trans-

port had recently been introduced; cable-hauled tramways, which in that city still exist to this very day. They appear frequently in a variety of American TV shows and feature films.

So, a Parliamentary Bill was introduced as early as 1883 for a similar system to operate in Edinburgh. This was seen as the answer to negotiating the steep hills which were prevalent in the city.

This first Bill, however, failed through opposition, not the least of which came from local residents in Newhaven, who did not wish to see trams run through their narrow streets. Dick Kerr & Co., the company behind the scheme, made various alterations to route suggestions and a second Bill was eventually accepted and the Edinburgh Northern Tramway Company was established on August 7 1884.

The construction of a cable tramway was, of course, considerably more difficult than the much simpler horse tramway system, for a third rail, or conduit, had to be laid to accommodate the moving cable which would haul the car along the rails. An engine house capable of providing the power to drive the cables was also necessary.

Track laying commenced in 1886, between Hanover Street and Goldenacre. Around the same time, the engine house and car depot were built in Henderson Row. This, the first of the cable routes, was opened for public use on January 28 1888.

Basically, an endless 3.5in circumference cable from the power house which powered the route, was led to the conduits via a series of pulleys. Each car was fitted with a 'gripper' which could be lowered and raised as necessary to grip the cable and provide traction. The company possessed 16 cars and speed was limited to 6 mph.

The fare from Hanover Street to Goldenacre was 3d (first class) and 2d (second class or 'outside') The same tickets could also be used for transfer to horse buses for continuation to Trinity or Granton, without extra charge. A second route, between Frederick Street and Comely Bank was opened in 1890. The Corporation subsequently obtained powers in 1893 to convert all existing

horse tramway routes to cable traction. Dick Kerr & Company, the contractors, formed a local company, The Edinburgh & District Tramways Company, to carry out the work. The laying of an extensive cable system in Edinburgh was an enormous task and many junctions must have given the planners and builders many a difficult problem to solve! At the same time, a horse tramway system was kept working along the same routes – a tremendous achievement.

The Edinburgh Northern Tramway Company was acquired by the Corporation in 1897 and the rolling stock was resold to the EDTC. The first cable route of this new company opened on October 26 1899, between Pilrig and Braid Hills.

Two new power stations were built at Shrubhill and Tollcross and (at the former) provision was made for cables to extend around Leith. Leith, however, was not interested in a cable system, it perhaps having an eye on future electrification; this commenced in August 1905.

Other routes of the 'new' cable system were opened, for example, to Gorgie and Murrayfield. An interesting feature was the length of cable used on the Nether Liberton to Shrubhill section. This was 33,500ft, the longest cable on the system. It was actually installed on April 18 1900.

By the end of 1900, most of the system had been converted from horse to cable working, only the Mound and Portobello routes had still to be introduced. These followed on September 11 1901 and May 1 1902 respectively. The cable system was then considered to be complete, it being 21.25 miles long.

During the early days the Company and the Corporation seemed to be in permanent dispute, the Company failing to make full rental payments being just one problem. Sunday-running without Corporation approval was another area of difficulty. However, the situation did eventually settle down, and harmony of a sort reigned for a period.

In January 1907 most of the routes were given numbers and these were displayed on a coloured oval board mounted on the upper deck rail. The numbers and colours were:

1: MURRAYFIELD AND NETHER LIBER-
TON: RED
2: PILRIG AND GORGIE: BLUE
3: ABBEYHILL AND ARDMILLAN TERRACE:
BLUE
4: PILRIG AND BRAID HILLS: GREEN
5: PILRIG AND MORNINGSIDE STATION:
GREEN
6: MARCHMONT AND CHURCH HILL:
WHITE
7: PILRIG AND NETHER LIBERTON: RED
8: PILRIG AND SALISBURY PLACE: RED

The Hanover Street, Comely Bank, Mound and Joppa routes never carried numbers. The light in the bulkhead saloon of the trams also showed the corresponding colour at night. This colour scheme continued, in a modified form, to the end of tramway working in 1956, apart from a break during the Second World War. A subsequent extension to Craiglockhart could have been the first electric tramway route in Edinburgh but due to various complications this was not to be and it too was a cable-operated service. Work

Above: An interesting scene inside Shrubhill Cable Power Station, showing the complicated arrangement of flywheels and pulleys, used to haul the cable through the street conduits. Opened in May 1899, it powered various cable routes. *LRT*.

Above: Although Edinburgh's tramways pursued a policy of trolley current collection, experiments with bow collectors (as used by Glasgow) were carried out in 1925 and, as shown here, by pantograph in 1933. Both these experiments were on the Portobello route; neither were a great success and car No. 73, shown here, only carried the pantograph from April until November of that year. Did the photographer really demolish part of the wall, to get his picture?! *LRT*.

11

commenced on conversion on August 24 1907 and the three horse cars operating the line were withdrawn. Thus ended horse tramway operation in Edinburgh.

Mention should be made of the short electrically operated line run by the Edinburgh & District Tramways Company from Ardmillan Terrace along Slateford Road which was opened in June 1910. The cars used to operate this route were housed at Shrubhill and had to be hauled to and from the electrified line by cable cars.

It was eventually realised that further extensions to the 25.75 mile cable system within the city would not be profitable. Other forms of traction were considered, including trolley buses, motor buses and various forms of tramway. Nearby, at Leith, the municipal authority was operating its electric cars very cheaply, no doubt much to the chagrin of Edinburgh Corporation. All manner of schemes and route extensions were planned around this period but the Great War, temporarily at least, caused them to be shelved.

The cable system suffered badly during the war period, with deteriorating rolling stock and many breakdowns. The general public became less than enthusiastic about their tramway service. However, the tramway company's days were numbered. The lease expired on June 30 1919 and the Corporation took over the following day. The Corporation was by this time committed to a programme of conversion to electric tramway operation; the route from Pilrig to Nether Liberton was considered the best first candidate for conversion. The Tramways Manager, Mr. R. Stuart Pilcher, who had been appointed a year earlier, planned to use as much existing equipment and rolling stock, suitably converted, as he could.

The Edinburgh Boundaries Extension and Tramways Act 1920 enabled extensions to the city boundary to be made and, perhaps more importantly, provided for the amalgamation of the Burgh of Leith with the City of Edinburgh, on November 2 1920.

Leith, of course, had been operating an electric system for many years. However, despite the commitment to electrification in Edinburgh, the 'Pilrig

A tram stop sign in Waterloo Place; cars ceased running from here in November 1954. *LRT.*

muddle', whereby the electric tram and cable car met but never actually joined up, was to continue for some time to come. At this time it was decided that the northern cable routes were worn-out and should be closed and (temporarily) be replaced by buses.

Henderson Row power station finally closed on January 24 1921 and subsequently became a bus garage. This had been the first power station to operate the cable trams having been opened in 1888. Unfortunately, most of the building has been demolished, although through persuasion and persistence it is good to know that the facade is to remain as a reminder to future generations of where the distinctive cable system began. It is also interesting that the power station lies just a few yards away from the last electric tram route,

the No. 23 (Morningside Station-Granton Road Station) on which services ended on November 16 1956.

Meanwhile, back to 1920; despite the fact that the cable system's days were numbered, services were improved and rolling stock modernised, mainly by the fitting of covers over the upper decks of the cars. Electric traction pole construction commenced in early 1922, between Pilrig and Nether Liberton, along Grange Road to Church Hill, Picardy Place to St. Andrew Street and London Road to Abbeyhill. The inauguration of the first new electric car to run between Leith and Edinburgh was on June 20 1922. Various dignitaries, naturally, were aboard this first car, but the occasion did not proceed quite as planned. Students from the University, aggrieved at not having been invited to ride on the car, hurled bags of flour at all and sundry! Remember, this was 1922 – perhaps things haven't changed all that much, after all! The public service followed during the course of the day and all the cable cars had been replaced on these converted sections by mid-afternoon. The cable finally stopped at 3.55 p.m.

At an official VIPs party at the City Chambers that night, one of the Councillor guests intimated that it was nice to see Edinburgh doing today what Leith had been doing for years!

Above: A solid-tyred Corporation Tramways vehicle at the scene of some welding operations during the early 1920s. A ride round the City in a vehicle with solid tyres on granite setts must have been an interesting experience! *LRT.*

Above: What appears to be an ex-works Metropolitan Cammell streamline car, No. 26, poses at Liberton terminus in 1935. This was one of a batch of 20 similar cars delivered in that year from outside contractors, the other contract builders being Hurst Nelson and English Electric. *LRT.*

Left: The close confines of Tollcross depot are clearly apparent as car No. 228 emerges into the sunshine for its next turn of duty, on service No. 28. This ornate building was demolished following closure (as a bus garage) in 1969. *Martin Jenkins/C.Bennett.*

The burghs might have amalgamated, but that did not mean that the old rivalries or animosities were at an end!

Conversion work now proceeded apace. Redundant cable cars were rebuilt for electric operation and wires and traction poles 'sprouted' in many parts of the city. However, one great problem remained. What to do about Princes Street? The very thought of poles and wires appearing along this sacred territory filled some people with horror. After much heart searching, it was agreed that centre poles should be erected. This caused great concern amongst some sections of the community and the issue reached no less an authority than the House of Commons. A Ministry of Transport public enquiry decreed that centre poles should be authorised. And so it was, and they remained until the end, in 1956. The change-over from cable to electric traction on Princes Street took place on Saturday/Sunday October 21/22 1922. 300 men were involved in what was a truly tremendous feat of conversion work. The first electric car ran down Princes Street at 9.30am on the Sunday morning.

Various other conversions and extensions to routes took place over the next few months. Tollcross

Power Station was closed and redundant cable cars were removed to Shrubhill for conversion. The Portobello route was the last cable-operated service. The last cable car ran on Saturday night June 23 1923, without any sort of farewell ceremony. An amazingly complicated system had finally come to an end with barely a second glance.

There is little left today to recall the cable era. A short length of track can be seen in Waterloo Place and, of course, the facade of the original depot building in Henderson Row remains at the time of writing. The final tramway routes to be electrified were the Northern and Mound. It will be recalled that these had been the first cable routes to be converted and had been replaced, temporarily, by buses. The No. 24 service, St. Andrew Street to Comely Bank, commenced on November 18 1923, whilst Service 23, from Goldenacre to Tollcross, began running on June 8 1924. Because of the particularly steep hills on these routes, cars were fitted with mechanically-operated track brakes and drivers were paid a halfpenny an hour extra, as it was considered they had a more arduous task. This bonus was, however, eventually withdrawn.

In the first five years of the Corporation Transport Department's life, much activity had taken place. All cable

routes had been converted to electric operation, most of the cable cars had been converted to electric operation and several extensions to existing routes had been added.

Most of the system's overhead was supported by span wires, either fixed to poles mounted in the pavement, or secured to wall rosettes affixed to buildings. These, unlike Glasgow, have now all disappeared, but close inspection today of many buildings still reveals the outline and bolt holes where they were once mounted. Some poles, now utilised as lampposts, still survive; St. Andrews Square is a good example. Centre poles were used in Princes Street, Leith Walk and Stanley Road.

Most busy junctions had automatic point controllers, fitted in the overhead wires. These enabled drivers to select (using their controllers) their desired direction of travel as they approached a junction. The exceptions were the West End and St. Andrew Street which were operated manually by a points boy. The junctions at the Post Office, Mound/Hanover Street and Frederick Street were controlled by a boy using an electric switch set in a box on the pavement. In 1925, rails were laid along George Street from Shandwick Place via Hope Street, Charlotte Square and into St. Andrews Square.

George Street was generally used as a relief from the much busier Princes Street and was mainly utilised by Service 2. Football specials also ran along here.

All the electric trams used trolley poles as the means of current collection, although an experiment with bow collectors (as used on Glasgow cars) and a pantograph was tried, but not pursued. Trolley wheels were used until the Second World War when conversion to a carbon insert 'skid', similar to those used on trolley buses, was introduced. These proved to be a great success inasmuch as they reduced arcing (a mortal sin in the blackout), were much more silent than wheels; they were also found to be considerably more economical.

In April 1926, the Council purchased the Industrial Hall in Annandale Street to use as a bus garage. Central Garage as it became known is, of course, still very much in use today. Henderson Row then ceased to be a bus garage and was subsequently to become the City Police Traffic Department garage. More tramway extensions took place over the next year or so, particularly at Corstorphine, Gorgie and Comely Bank.

Musselburgh Tramways Company were having problems around this time and gave up its tramway operation in favour of buses. The line beyond Levanhall to Port Seton was abandoned. After some wrangling, Edinburgh finally took over the line to Levanhall on April 25 1932. Much renewal and reconstruction followed to improve the service over the old company lines.

A further extension of the Corstorphine route to North Gyle farm was opened for public use on July 1 1934.

On the occasion of the royal visit of the Duke and Duchess of York on May 11 1935, a tradition began which was to last until the very end of tramway operation. This was the affixing of coloured pennants (generally three) to the trolley ropes of all cars. During all such future visits (and also at Festival periods) this pleasant touch of colour was perpetuated and appreciated. Many of the photographs in this book clearly show these pennants fluttering in the

Above: A most unfortunate accident occured at Morningside station one morning in September 1956, involving two trams, Nos. 225 and 189, which turned across the other car's path. Domed-roof standard car No. 225 (the last car to be built, in 1950) and had been selected for preservation. However, it was considered too badly damaged to be repaired at this late stage. Sister car 189, also seen here, was badly damaged and was scrapped immediately. Car No. 172, the second choice, had already been repainted for the final week of operation, so car No. 35 was chosen for preservation, it being in the best condition of the remaining cars. *D. Hunt.*

seemingly endless breeze which the city is equally famous for.

An extension up to Fairmilehead from Braids was opened on April 19 1936, and this remained almost to the end of tramway operation.

What proved to be the final piece of tramway extension was yet another lengthening of the Corstorphine route through to the Maybury, opened on February 14 1937.

Other planned extensions from Liberton to Kaimes and along Ferry Road to Crewe Road Toll were never built, mainly as a result of the war. A start had been made on the Crewe Road Toll link, but was abandoned; there had in any event been some inter-Council disagreement as to whether to proceed with a tram route or run a bus service instead. Wartime Edinburgh was, certainly initially, much the same as everywhere else in the UK, with enforced blackout causing much inconvenience. Trams ran without some lamps, headlights were dimmed, destination screens were made as difficult as possible to read and route colour symbols were suspended.

Services were, however, more or less maintained, with track work and some overhead wire renewal taking place mainly during daylight hours.

With many men away from home serving in the armed forces, conductresses were employed from the end of May 1941, and were to be a feature on the trams until they were scrapped.

In 1942, the Ministry of War Transport requested the number of stopping places be reduced to minimise wear and tear. This resulted in 120 stops being removed – some probably were never reinstated. Edinburgh came through the war relatively unscathed and, towards 1945, various relaxations were permitted – particularly in allowing better lighting on the cars. After the celebration of Victory in Europe day in May 1945, all services started to rapidly get back to normal, with full lighting restored; this was no doubt received with much relief by crews and passengers alike.

The commencement of tram abandonment (although it was probably not recognised as such at the time) was the withdrawal of Service 18 and its replacement by buses. This took place on March 26 1950. Although this was the first service to be withdrawn, no actual rails were lifted – this did not happen until three years later. In June 1950, the Transport Manager, W. M. Little, put forward a proposal that no more extensions to the existing tramway system be undertaken and that 25% of the system should actually be scrapped. Two Council Committees agreed with his proposal. However, the full Council rejected it. News of this proposal was inevitably 'leaked' to the press and public in general, prompting considerable alarm. The proposals were raised again later in the year and were finally passed by the Council on November 2.

However, for the moment, the system remained intact with various improvements being undertaken; Princes Street was resurfaced, new automatic point controllers were installed at the Mound and Hanover Street. The equipment at Frederick Street/Princes Street was something of a semi-automatic innovation with the driver operating a manual switch on the centre pole for cars going to Comely Bank. The junction at the Post Office continued to be a manual operation but as a small concession to the operation, the switch gear was enclosed in a kiosk mounted on the pavement by the statue of the Duke of Wellington.

In September 1951, the tram routes proposed for conversion to bus operation were announced. They were those to Comely Bank, Slateford and Stenhouse. Around this time, the Council was looking for ways to increase revenue, other than unpopular fare increases. So, agreement was reached with an advertising agency, namely Cowans, to utilise the upper deck side panels of buses and trams, for the display of advertisements. Many people felt this practice was 'degrading' and certainly not suitable for the Scottish capital.

However, the scheme went ahead and adverts began appearing during 1952. These were tastefully applied, were always painted (no paper and paste here!) and really did not detract unduly from the appearance of the buses and trams. Goodness knows what the local 'worthies' of 1952 would have made of today's garish vinyl adverts appearing on a much greater area of the vehicle than would have been tolerated then – and that's before we consider the 'all-over' bus adverts! Whatever, advertising certainly brought in considerable extra revenue, as indeed it still does today!

The city's population was at this time becoming increasingly aware of the tram replacement programme and many letters of protest appeared in the press. Councillors were left in no doubt that, in general, the feeling was that the trams should remain at work! A browse through copies of the *Evening News* for this period makes interesting reading. The tram issue, from the Council's point of view, became intensely political and generated bitter divisions. However, as planned, the first tram route to be withdrawn was Service 24, to Comely Bank which was replaced, initially, by single deck buses, on June 1 1952. It soon became apparent that the ruling body of the Council had become fiercely 'anti-tram' and wanted to be rid of the whole system as soon as possible. Any criticism was denounced as reactionary and it was made clear that no notice should be taken of newspaper correspondence. Those in government knew better than those who had elected them and the order of the day was to ignore all opposition and forge ahead regardless.

The inevitable came to pass: an announcement that the whole system was to be abandoned was made public on July 15 1952 and it was passed in Council by 31 votes to 21 on September 25 of the same year. This decision caused widespread public disquiet and much controversy over a lengthy period. There was a public meeting in the Central Hall, which unanimously demanded the Council rescind their proposals. The Council paid not the slightest heed to this (or any other protestations) and even produced a set of 'contrived' figures to prove the trams were losing money far more heavily than the buses. These were later admitted to be incorrect. Due to continuing problems with finances, a further round of fare increases (adding insult to injury) took place on the December 7 1952 when the minimum fare was increased to 2d.

Also during this same month the No. 2 service (which ran from Stenhouse to Granton) was withdrawn. This was the only regular service which used George Street, thus enabling the dismantling of the overhead and lifting of rails to take place. However, this did not actually happen until March the following year. Routes 3 and 4 were converted to bus operation in March and May

Left: A workshop view at Shrubhill works, clearly showing the lineshaft and belt drive to the lathes and other machine tools. The frame of a truck is being repaired, together with wheels, gearing and tyres. *LRT.*

1953 respectively and Gorgie Depot was converted to a bus garage.

Around about this time, 60 surplus cars were sold to James Connell, of Coatbridge, for scrap. This company enjoyed a profitable period over the next three years by breaking-up the remaining fleet of trams. The cars for scrap, certainly in the early stages of the system's abandonment, were driven under their own power out to the Corstorphine terminus at the Maybury, loaded on to one of Connell's specially adapted vehicles and then driven away. This practice continued until shortly after the Corstorphine services (Nos. 1, 12, 25 and 26) were withdrawn, by July 1954. Thereafter, loading for the sad last journey, was undertaken in North Junction Street and finally at Shrubhill itself.

For the remainder of 1954 and throughout 1955, tram services were withdrawn at a relentless pace. It was a sad time for those who believed that electric tramways were a sound method of public transport. More than 30 years later, belated (but still welcome!) municipal enthusiasm for Light Rail Transit systems (trams by any other name) has proved the sound thinking of the pro-tram lobby.

At the beginning of 1956, the following services remained operative: 6, 7, 11, 13, 14, 16, 17, 19, 23 and 28, serving such areas as Fairmilehead, Liberton, Grange, Marchmont, Ferry Road, Granton and Seafield. Leith depot was closed to trams on May 5 1956, leaving just Tollcross to soldier on until the end.

Princes Street had undergone major resurfacing work over the year and to enable the latter part, between St. Andrew Street and the Post Office, to be finished, the surviving routes, 11, 13, 14 and 28 were diverted via York Place to join the Service 16 route. The last trams to use the bridges ran on June 16 when Services 13 and 14 (the Granton Circle via Grange and Church Hill) were withdrawn. The system's total abandonment was now looming ever closer and Service 11 (Fairmilehead to Stanley Road)and Service 16 (Fairmilehead to Granton) were withdrawn on Wednesday September 12 1956. This meant that Routes 23 (Morningside Station and Granton Road Station via Hanover Street) and 28 (Braids to Stanley Road via York Place and Pilrig Street) were now the only survivors.

Despite the fact that the Suez crisis had developed and an oil shortage was looming, no stay of execution was forthcoming, despite the threat of fuel shortages which would inevitably affect the availability and economics of motor bus operation. The date for the final services was set as Friday November 16 1956. During the last week of operation, a specially decorated car No. 172, toured what remained of the system and many hundreds of photographs were taken, not only by enthusiasts but also by residents alike, who wished to preserve the memory of the trams for future generations to see.

Enormous crowds turned out on the sad last night, to witness the passing of an era. Ten cars had made their way to Braids to be joined at Morningside Station by car No. 217, carrying the official party. Large crowds lined virtually the whole route as the cars, pennants proudly fluttering from their trolley ropes, made their way slowly through Tollcross, along Lauriston Place and down the Mound. At the foot of the Mound, an official presentation was made by the Lady Provost to three drivers, namely James Pryde (on car No. 88) William Moffatt (on the decorated car No. 172) and James Kay (on No. 217).

This deed done, the cars made their very last journey, along Princes Street, into St. Andrews Square, York Place and, finally, Leith Walk. They entered Shrubhill at 9.30pm, bringing 85 years of tramway history to a dignified close. Many thought at the time that a mistake had been made in disposing of the trams – many more probably think the same today, and as this book went to press, speculation about a new, modern light railway (tramway!) for the city prompts hope that those in authority are finally in agreement.

A report in the following night's *Evening News* gave a full account of the proceedings of the last run under the headline 'All Edinburgh goes gay'. They'd never do it today!

Frederick Street in 1953. The first tram route to be withdrawn was Service 24, from Waverley to Comely Bank. This ceased on May 31 1952, although the overhead equipment and track were not removed until the following year. As tram routes were replaced over the following three years, rails were lifted and ultimately tarmac replaced the setts. In Frederick Street, however, as the rails were removed, the setts were replaced and where the rails had been the setts were refitted in the opposite direction to the established pattern, leaving a permanent reminder of the tramway. The Leyland *Titan* bus in the background is working on tram replacement service No. 29. *LRT.*

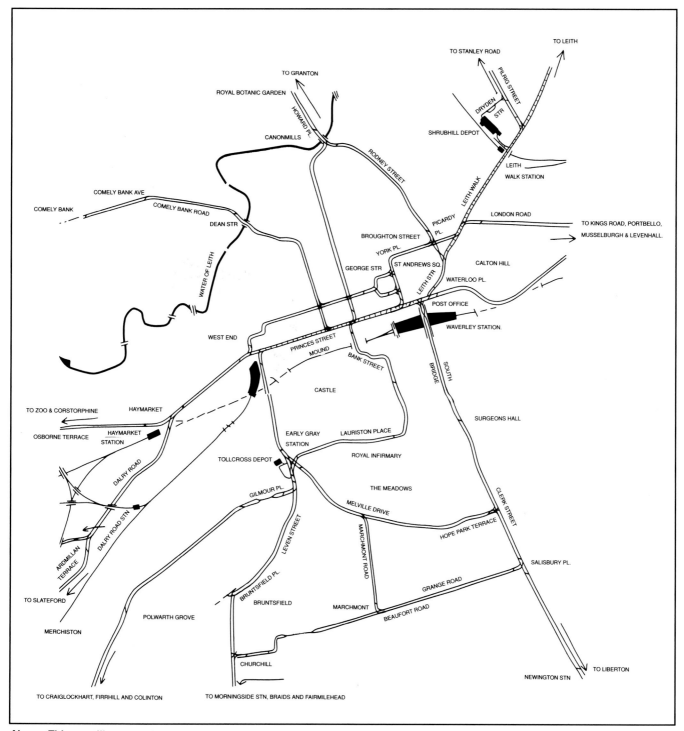

Above: This map illustrates the general layout of Edinburgh's tramways in the centre and inner city areas. Detail alterations (such as the removal of crossovers and junctions) were implemented at various times and are not recorded here.

Above: A familiar scene at Tollcross on August 11 1953. Wooden-bodied Standard car No. 159 clatters over the points en route to Bernard Street, Leith, as a policeman directs traffic at this busy junction. The Methodist Central Hall, built between 1899 and 1901, still stands today, though in a somewhat cleaner condition. Flemings Stores have now departed and this part of the building is now the Crosswinds Community Centre. All the buildings on the right have been demolished and (at the time of going to press) the site was due to host a new shopping development. *R. Wiseman.*

Right: Tollcross, looking along Home Street, with the Barclay Bruntsfield Church in the background. Wooden-bodied Standard car No.198 has just descended Lauriston Place and is on its way to Morningside Station, on Service 23. A good example of an illuminated tram stop post can clearly be seen alongside the small boy looking curiously at the photographer! The *Cameo Cinema* is still there today. *A. K. Terry.*

Left, upper: Domed-roof Standard Car 204 swings onto the single track of West Tollcross, bound for the Depot after a spell of duty on August 11 1953. The conductress can be seen on the platform step, trolley rope in hand, ready to guide the car into the Depot. *R. Wiseman.*

Left, lower: Brougham Street, Tollcross, is the setting for this fine view. Car No. 211 is about to reverse on the crossover, on Service 19. This normally ran to Craigentinny Avenue, but on this occasion it was a short working to the foot of Leith Walk. This part of Tollcross looks much the same today, although the chimney of the power station (seen above the roof of the Central Hall) has now gone, together with the stone setts and tram track.
The power station was built by Dick Kerr and Company in 1896-98 for the then new cable-worked tram system. The first cable car to be used by the public ran on October 26 1899. Electric working took over in Edinburgh from 1922. Tollcross Depot housed trams until the final day of operation, on November 16 1956. The Depot was converted as a bus garage until it finally closed on September 13 1969. The SMT Coach in this scene is a Duple-bodied AEC vehicle. These green and cream vehicles were a common sight in the City for many years. Note the British Linen Bank (now The Bank of Scotland) on the left; also the large pram in the middle distance, on the right. Today's pushchairs are certainly easier to handle! *John Fozard Collection.*

Facing page, upper: Lothian Road, near the Usher Hall, looking towards the West End, in 1954. Princes Street (the Caledonian station) and Caledonian Hotel dominates the centre and left background. The last train ran from here on September 6 1965. The Hotel, designed by J.M. Dick Peddie and George Washinton Browne, was built over the station, which had opened in the 1880s. The car showroom on the left (note also the 'Guinness for strength' poster!) has now gone, the area forming part of Festival Square, overlooked by the 1982 Sheraton Hotel. The *Caley Cinema* on the right survives today, although it is now known as The Amphitheatre (a nightclub). There are six domed-roof standard cars visible (all heading towards the photographer) with 224 and 82 leading the pack. There are many interesting vehicles in the scene, including a Ford *Prefect*, a Riley, a Wolseley and a Morris GPO telephone van, not to mention a rather splendid motorcycle. *LRT.*

Facing page, lower: A scene which has changed almost beyond recognition. This is the foot of Leith Street, looking down Broughton Street. The Theatre Royal with a capacity of 1,500 (on the left, with a canopy over the pavement) was destroyed by fire in 1946; the site was subsequently sold to the Roman Catholic Church for £10,000 in 1950. The Morris 'J' Van in the foreground was owned by Hoys, who specialised in prams and who also had branches in Kirkcaldy and Dunfermline. The Austin heavy chassis van parked beyond at the kerbside was owned by Millers, the Wireless company. This block was demolished in 1969, to make way for a major road scheme (part of which involved a tunnel entrance under the St James Centre) and a massive roundabout, once home to an ultimately unpopular abstract sculpture. *LRT.*

Right, upper and lower: Another scene which has been utterly transformed today. This is the Junction of Broughton Street and Leith Street. Domed-roof Standard car No. 213 is working route 10 to Granton, passing Metro-Cammell car No. 26, en route for Braids on the 28 service. At the time of going to press, the new Hospitality Inn complex was taking shape on the left, where in 1954, the shops included Alexander's, Halford's and David Murray's fancy goods establishment. Across the street, the Hill Brothers pawnbroker provided an essential service, loaning cash in return for the surety of jewellery and other valuables. Forfeited pledges, from those who could not repay their debts, could be bought cheaply. This block was redeveloped in 1973. Note the young man on the right, neatly attired in gaberdine 'mac' and grey school knee-socks – not to mention the 'Brylcreemed' short-back-and-sides! Note also the complete lack of litter. *LRT.*

Above: A latter-day view of Leith Street, on September 12 1989, showing the almost complete transformation of the scene. The St James's Centre and Lewis's now occupy the right-hand side of the view. *Nigel Harris.*

Left: A rare view: Car No. 337 is on its way to Granton in August 1952, in George Street. Service No. 2 alone used this street and was one of the first tram routes to be withdrawn, in December 1952. The statue of William Pitt the Younger (erected by Francis Chantrey, in 1833) gazes down Frederick Street. The statues along George Street have long been the subject of much debate and calls for their removal, because of the way they are said to impede traffic flow. They resolutely survive today. An interesting array of cars in the scene includes a Ford V8 *Pilot*, two Austin *Devon* saloons and a Sunbeam Talbot. The large building on the left, built in 1903-1904 for the Professional and Civil Service Supply Association, was altered in 1936 by the Scottish Co-operative Wholesale Society and altered yet again in the 1970s to become Edinburgh's only branch of the National Westminster Bank. Note also Hardy's Fish Shop on the right. *R. Wiseman.*

Above: A classic view of Princes Street, featuring a variety of trams, in 1953. Many of Edinburgh's famous landmarks are visible, with the Castle dominating the scene to the left. The Royal Academy and the smoke-blackened bulk of the Caledonian Hotel also feature strongly. The spires of the Cathedral of St Mary stand out starkly against the sky in the background. The Scott Monument, from which the photograph was taken, was designed by George Meikle Kemp in 1844. The statue of Scott (by Sir John Steell) was installed in 1846. *Courtesy British Railways.*

Right: The familiar skyline of the old town dominates the scene on a sunny day in April 1955, as Shrubhill's Domed-roof Standard Car No. 69 climbs the Mound, on its way to Craiglockhart, on service 27. This car was the prototype of this style of tram, of which a total of 84 examples were built at Shrubhill between 1934 and 1950. In my view, these were superbly-designed cars in every way. Their clean lines and perfect proportions made them so much a part of the Edinburgh scene. It is fortunate, if not remarkable, that No. 35 survived, as a preserved example. Note the elaborate poles supporting the span wires. These appear to have recently been repainted. *David Packer Collection.*

Left: Domed-roof Standard car No. 235 reaches the summit of the long climb up Pitt Street and Dundas Street and passes the statue of George IV at the junction of George Street. This statue, by Francis Chantrey, was erected in 1831 to commemorate the King's visit to the capital in 1822. Note the flower boxes surrounding the plinth – probably placed in connection with the annual Festival. *A. K. Terry.*

Below: The view from Register House, looking along North Bridge, on July 3 1954. Wooden-bodied Standard car No. 46 is about to swing right along Leith Street, en route to Granton Square. Although not apparent in this picture, this was an extremely busy tramway junction, controlled from a special pointsbox some way to the left of the Wellington Statue, which was erected in 1852. The Duke of Wellington 'sat' for John Steell, the designer, in 1848. It was erected by James Gowan, on a red granite pedestal designed by David Bryce. "The Iron Duke in Bronze by Steell" has long been a nickname for the statue. The present structure of North Bridge dates from 1894-97 when it replaced a 1772 version, which had been widened in 1873. The bridge was rebuilt to facilitate the Waverley station scheme. *LRT.*

Above: The east end of Princes Street, in 1954. Standard car No. 214 is heading for Church Hill, surrounded by an interesting variety of vehicles, including a 1947 Beardmore taxi, a Hillman military van, a Jowett *Javelin* and a pre-war Austin 4 saloon. During excavations at this location in June 1989, relics of cable tram tracks and haulage conduit were revealed. The skyline has changed relatively little in the intervening years; Elliott's bookshop became part of the Menzies empire some years ago. *David Packer Collection.*

Right: Lauriston Place, outside the Royal Infirmary. Car 236 is operating the very short working between Hanover Street and the Infirmary. The Conductress has turned the trolley and can clearly be seen still grasping the rope until the car has completed its reversal. Other vehicles in this August 8 1956 scene, include an Austin FX2 taxi and a Volkswagen Beetle. A partially obscured sign on the left proclaims the availability of artificial limbs. *A. K. Terry.*

A scene which has changed considerably since this picture was taken in 1954. The lorry on the right is encroaching on the trams right of way, causing a backlog of at least six trams in Leith Street. The buildings on the left were swept away as part of the St. James Centre re-development, planned in 1964 and completed in 1970. This Centre was actually built behind the old shops, which were then demolished, and it came as something of a shock to Edinburgh folk when it was finally revealed. A few buildings survived, although these were also originally scheduled for demolition. They date from 1800 and were renovated in 1979-81 as housing and shops. Other buildings were demolished in 1973, ostensibly to make way for the new BBC Broadcasting House, but this did not materialise and the site was a car park for many years. The Hospitality Inn is now under construction. Two branches of H. Samuel within a few yards of each other were situated on the left hand side of the street. The 'H' incidentally stands for Henrietta, probably a little-known fact! Leith Street also had some famous pubs, alas no more, such as the Thistle Inn, The Argyll Bar, Fairlies and the Register Tap. However, the Black Bull, partially at least, re-opened as a wine bar down the steps at the side of Calton Road. *David Packer Collection.*

Above: A once-familiar view of Tollcross, in the summer of 1956, as car No. 88 approaches a policeman on point duty at the road junction. In Lauriston Place, the building carrying the *Ekco* advertisement is now a car park, adjacent to Goldberg's store. *D.G.Clark.*

Above, right: This advertisement was used by the Corporation Transport Department for many years, to promote its special tours. The Arthur's Seat tour (including the Royal Mile and King's Park, September 30-June 1 only) took about 40 minutes, for a fare of one shilling (5p)! *Michael Ashworth Collection.*

Right: A listing of tramway routes, as detailed in the the Transport Department's official map of 1951. *Michael Ashworth Collection.*

Far right: A fine view of Princes Street, towards the end of tramway operations, in 1956. Car Nos. 72, 105 and 45 are shown heading east, crossing the junction at the foot of the Mound. Although buses had almost taken over by this time, the trams are still dominating the scene. *D.G.Clark.*

TRAMWAY ROUTES

Service No.	ROUTE	Route Colour	Service No.	ROUTE	Route Colour
1	Liberton and Corstorphine	Red Blue	15	Braids and King's Road *via* York Place and London Road	Green White
2	Granton and Stenhouse *via* York Place and George Street	Blue	16	Fairmilehead and Granton Square *via* York Pl., Leith Walk & Junction St.	Green
3	Newington Stn. and Stenhouse *via* Princes Street	Blue White	17	Newington Stn. & Granton Square *via* Bernard Street	White
4	Piershill and Slateford *via* London Road and Princes Street	White Blue	19	Craigentinny Ave. No. & Tollcross *via* Bridges and Melville Drive	Green Red
5	Morningside Stn., Salisbury and Piershill *via* Grange Road and Bridges	Red Green	20	Edinburgh G.P.O., Portobello and Joppa	Red
6	Marchmont Circle (Either Direction) P.O., Marchmont, West End	White Red	21	Edinburgh G.P.O., Portobello, Musselburgh and Levenhall	Green
7	Liberton and Stanley Road *via* Junction Street	Red	23	Granton Rd. Stn., Tollcross, Bruntsfield & Morningside *via* Mound	Green Yellow
8	Granton Sq. and Newington Stn. *via* Broughton St.	Red Yellow	24	Waverley, Stockbridge and Comely Bank *via* Frederick Street	Red
9	Granton Square and Colinton *via* Broughton St.	Yellow	25	Drum Brae South and King's Road *via* York Place and Leith Walk	Blue Yellow
10	Bernard Street and Colinton	White Yellow	26	Piershill and Drum Brae South *via* London Road and Princes Street	Blue Red
11	Fairmilehead and Stanley Road *via* Pilrig Street	Red White	27	Granton Rd. Stn., and Firrhill *via* Mound and Lauriston	Yellow Red
12	Corstorphine, King's Road and Joppa *via* Leith & Seafield	Yellow Blue	28	Braids and Stanley Road *via* Pilrig Street	Blue Green
13	Churchhill and Granton Circle *via* Pilrig Street	White Green			
14	Churchhill and Granton Circle *via* Bernard Street	Yellow Green			

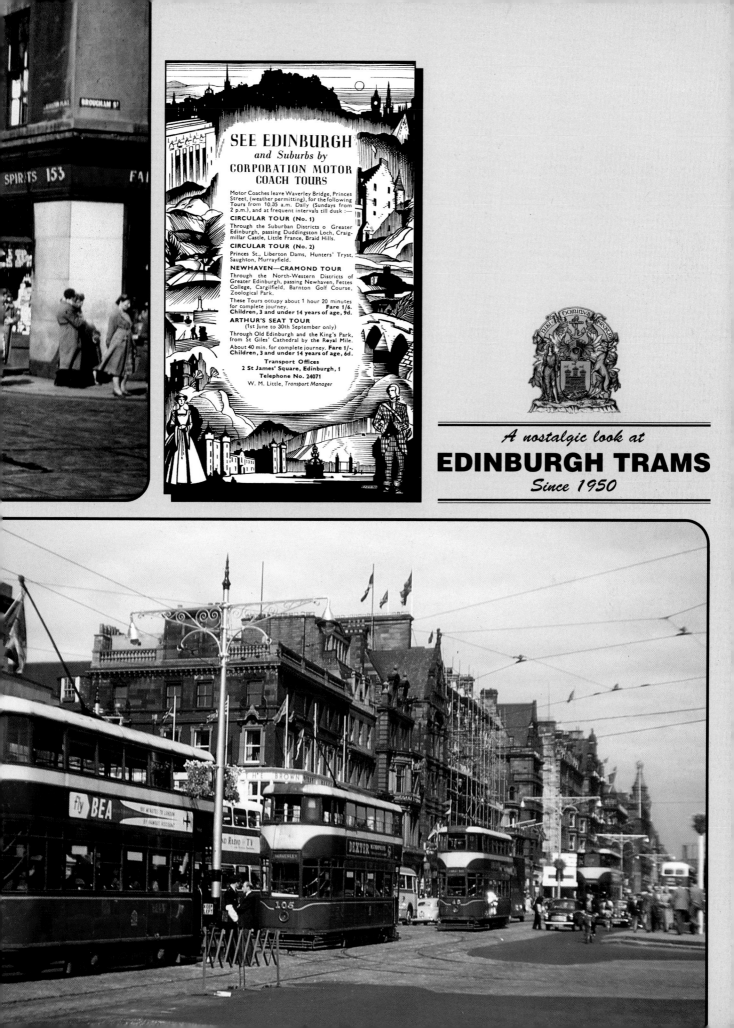

A nostalgic look at

EDINBURGH TRAMS
Since 1950

Right: The single track section in Gilmore Place is host to Car No. 33 on its way to Colinton on August 11 1953. The sign on the wall on the right proclaims that pleasure boats on the Canal could be hired, whilst J. & J. Cowie (Painters, Paperhangers, Grainers and signwriters) were also promoting their services. Don't miss the tiny motorised ice cream vehicle, also making its way towards the camera. *R. Wiseman.*

Below: A pleasant summers evening in 1953 finds wooden-bodied Standard car No. 65 passing Leamington Terrace.The car has had its side-panel painted white, ready for the signwriter to apply a new advertisement. This practice had started on the city's trams and buses earlier the previous year. An Austin A35 is overtaking the tram. *David Packer Collection.*

Left: It's August 1 1953 in Nicholson Street and tram No. 120 is heading towards Morningside Station on Service No 5, having left Piershill some little while earlier. This service ran via London Rd, the Bridges, Grange Rd, Church Hill and Morningside Road; it was replaced by a bus service with the same number on October 31 1954. Here we see a veritable medley of late 18th and early 19th century buildings with an accompanying variety of shops. Redevelopment took place between 1979 and 1981, when some facades survived, whilst others were rebuilt . A Bedford/Duple coach, so common in the 1950s but now museum pieces, rumbles over the setts behind No. 120. Note the bare-headed motorcyclists and pillion passengers, for these were the days before crash helmets were mandatory. *R. Wiseman.*

Right: Metropolitan-Cammell steel Car No. 260 passes Bruntsfield Links in 1954. This scene has changed little over the years and the spire of Barclay Brunstfield Church still dominates the background. This Church was designed by Frederick T. Pilkington and was built between 1862 and 1864. A local worthy, Miss Mary Barclay bequeathed the money to build the church – hence its name. One of the slatted Lucarnes (small spires in the main spire) was blown down in 1969 and all four were subsequently replaced in grey fibreglass. *LRT.*

Left: A very pleasant setting in Bruntsfield Place, as car No.210 passes the Links, on its way to Fairmilehead. This car was built in 1947, spent all its life allocated to Tollcross Depot and survived until the end of tramway operations, in 1956. The row of villas on the left was built in 1826-27. The name Ediswan, as seen on the side of No. 210, was founded in 1881, as the Edison and Swan United Electric Light Company, a merger of Swan and Edison – formerly rival concerns. *David Packer Collection.*

Right: Four soldiers pass domed-roof Standard car No. 204, which is about to reverse (at Warriston Place) on a short working back to Craiglockhart. The route number is not identifiable, but is probably 27. Further down the street is car No. 68. Today, a new building stands on the site of Tanfield, which is now a major development area. Tanfield was the early home of the two rival 1820s gas companies, one of which was the Oil Gas Company (Sir Walter Scott was Chairman); the company failed in 1839 and the building became Tanfield Hall, scene of the First Free Church Assembly in 1839. *David Packer Collection.*

Left: The familiar location of Canonmills, in March 1954, as car No. 137 heads for Granton Road station, having travelled from Craiglockart on Service 27. An unidentified Standard car is passing over the junction, to head along Rodney Street and Broughton Street. The clock is an interesting feature; erected in 1947, it was provided (so the story goes!) in an attempt to encourage tram crews to keep better time! The police box on the left is one of many similar survivors in the city today, some as, in this case, still carrying an air raid siren. T & J Bernard were brewers at Slateford. The firm was taken over by S & N in 1960. *LRT.*

Below: A busy scene in South Bridge, at the Chambers Street Junction. Hurst Nelson streamlined car No. 13 ambles along on its journey from Liberton to Stanley Road, Newhaven. The destination 'Stanley Road' was something of a misnomer, as the actual terminus was at the foot of neighbouring Craighall Road. It was moved to this location on October 17 1949 and provided a service for Craighall Road after an interval of more than 30 years, an earlier service (provided by Leith Corporation) having been withdrawn in 1917. However, destination blinds were never altered. The spire in the background is the Tron Kirk, this was built in 1636-47 by John Mylne Jnr to house a congregation displaced from St Giles, when this church (which had previously housed three congregations) became a Cathedral. The Tron was shortened and lost its South Aisle in the reconstruction of 1785-87, to form South Bridge and Hunter Square. The Steeple was burned in a fire of 1824 and was replaced in 1828-29. The exterior of the church was restored in 1973-75 (by Andrew Renton) and the interior gutted revealing archaeological remains of Marlins Wynd, an earlier thoroughfare. Now empty for many years, it was once mooted as a prospective tourist information centre. *LRT.*

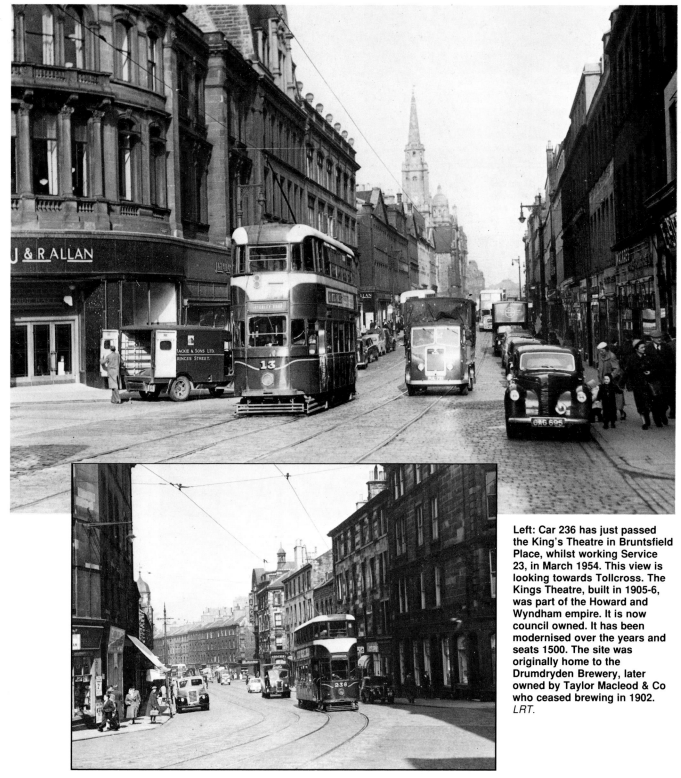

Left: Car 236 has just passed the King's Theatre in Bruntsfield Place, whilst working Service 23, in March 1954. This view is looking towards Tollcross. The Kings Theatre, built in 1905-6, was part of the Howard and Wyndham empire. It is now council owned. It has been modernised over the years and seats 1500. The site was originally home to the Drumdryden Brewery, later owned by Taylor Macleod & Co who ceased brewing in 1902. *LRT.*

Right: An attractive three-quarter view of car No. 39, turning out of Pilrig Street, to join the seemingly endless procession of cars in Leith Walk, including sister car No. 189. This was the spot where chaos reigned for many years when passengers from Leith had to change from one form of traction to another, initially from one company's horse-drawn cars to its neighbour's horse cars, and subsequently from Leith electric cars to Edinburgh cable trams. *A.K. Terry.*

Below: Leith Walk, with The Albert Bar in the background, as Metro-Cammell streamlined car No. 16 passes the entrance to Shrubhill Works, on its way to Granton. The City Fruit shop and the tram are both advertising Heinz Products; tomato soup and tomato ketchup. Both products are, of course, still with us today. Also advertised on the fruit shop window are black grapes at 1s.8d (about 8p) per pound. *David Packer.*

SUBURBS AND BEYOND

Left: Well-filled ex-Manchester 'Pilcher' Car No. 409 passes the junction of Northfield Broadway on August 2 1953, on its way to Levenhall. The white 'slip board' (a common sight on Edinburgh's trams) gave various 'via' descriptions to the car's route. This example proclaims: 'To and from Portobello Beach and Pool'. *R. Wiseman.*

Above: A pleasant view taken of Northfield Broadway, looking towards Piersfield Terrace, with two wooden standard cars prominent. An unidentified car is seen in broadside, heading into the city, whilst No. 292 is working on Service 5, to Morningside Station. Both are extolling the virtues of Bells Whisky. This picture was taken on October 30 1954, the last day in operation for Service 5. The trolley-head locating plate, which made it easier to find the wire when trolley turning in the dark, can clearly be seen. These were a feature at all terminals in the latter years of tramway operation. This scene has changed little over the years; Bannerman's Butchers shop was still there in 1989, though seemingly abandoned at the time of writing. *LRT.*

Left: Wooden-bodied Standard car No. 368 climbs Upper Granton Road on the long journey back to Colinton, as a cross-city freight train steams away from Granton Harbour. *The Wardie Hotel* is still there today; it dates from 1881. At the time of going to press, plans were afoot to start a massive infill of the sea here, for development. This has, not un-naturally, upset the local population, who formed the Wardie Bay Action Group to fight the proposal. *David Packer Collection.*

Above: The easily recognisable location of Trinity Bridge – which remains remarkably unchanged today, although the trams and their track are long gone. This track was part of the Leith Corporation System and opened in May 1909. Due to the awkwardness of the 'S' bend, which made it impossible for drivers to see approaching traffic, this was a single line, controlled by signals. You can almost hear the sound of squealing flanges as car No. 159 negotiates the curves on its way to Newington station. Note that the conductor has forgotten to change the rear screen – it still reads 'Granton.' The adverts are interesting: Kit Kat, incidentally, was launched in 1935 as Chocolate Crisp. Surf washing powder is still with us today as, of course, is The *Evening News*. This newspaper, founded in 1873, was merged with The *Evening Despatch* (founded 1866) in 1963 as part of a complex deal with Provincial Newspapers/Thompsons. The *Despatch* was the sister paper to The *Scotsman*. *David Packer.*

Left: The foot of Craighall Road, the 'Stanley Road' terminus, where services Nos. 7, 11 and 28 reversed. Seen here are cars Nos. 25, 165 and, in the background, 35 (now preserved). The small building in the background (above the heads of the people in the tram queue) was there for the 'convenience' (!) of staff. It remains today, but in a somewhat derelict condition. *David Packer.*

Left: The junction of Pilrig Street, Bonnington Road, Newhaven Road and Broughton Road, at the railway overbridge on April 29 1954. Wooden-bodied Standard car No. 146 heads for Granton, whilst working Service No. 13. The old Toll Bar remains to this day, but the railway bridge has, however, gone. The line was part of the South Leith Caledonian link, constructed around 1899 and opened in 1903. It was singled in 1917 and finally closed in the 1960s. The sign on the bridge reads: 'Danger Do Not Touch The Wires!' On the right, a workman is seemingly helping keep the streets clean. *R. Wiseman.*

Right: A modern-day view of the same location, in September 1989, showing how the scene has changed in the intervening years. *Nigel Harris.*

Left: A cold winters day in February 1954 in Newhaven Road. English Electric-built streamlined car No. 20, followed by domed-roof Standard car No. 63, are heading for Liberton and Fairmilehead respectively. The side-bracketed suspension poles were uncommon on the system and, as can clearly be seen, forced the trolley arm away from a central position. This also happened at various other places, particularly where centre poles were used. Already, the ornate lamp posts in the picture are being replaced by functional (though aesthetically dreadful) concrete versions. These, in turn, have now also been replaced. *LRT.*

Above: An excellent three-quarter view of immaculate car No. 202 turning from Ferry Road into Newhaven Road on August 11 1953. The photograph clearly shows the busy junction, with its web of wires and rails. The noise of many four-wheeled cars clattering over the rail joints must have been an impressive and characteristic aspect of city life. To the left of the church spire in the background can be seen the Automatic Point Changers (the 'blob' in the overhead wire). The general rule for crossing and turning at tramway junctions was to coast for straight-ahead running, or give two notches of power to change the points to deviate to right or left. Car No. 202 is carrying a very common advert of the period for Westons Biscuits: "Save pence per pound". Westons were originally sited in Slateford Road, under the Locarno Ballroom. The company was relocated in Sighthill but opened under the Burton name. Their maroon and red Dodge and Bedford vans were a familiar sight in the city. *R. Wiseman.*

Left: Although the general scene has changed little since this photograph was taken at Newington station, near Mayfield Gardens, during 1954, the volume of traffic now passing this spot has increased manyfold. Wooden-bodied Standard car No. 356 is seen here reversing, whilst working on Service 8, back to Granton. The stone setts have long since gone, as has Newington station. This closed on September 10 1962, together with the other stations on the suburban circle. *LRT.*

Below: Wooden Standard car No. 356 is pictured at the foot of Leith Walk as it clatters over the junction to run down Constitution Street and on to Granton. This was Service 17, from Newington Station, which last ran on March 10 1956. Above the tram's roof can be seen part of the word 'Theatre'; this was the Gaiety, which was off to the left in Kirkgate. The F. W. Woolworth store survives today. *David Packer Collection.*

Above: The terminus for Service 19 at Craigentinny Avenue, as English Electric streamlined car No. 24 is about to reverse on the crossover, before running back to Tollcross. This gives another good example of the trolley head locating plate – a wartime innovation to help crews 'find the wire' in the blackout. *LRT.*

Above: June 1954 in Commercial Street, Leith, looking towards Bernard Street. It is close to the North British (LNER) North Leith Station (built 1840), which closed to passengers on June 16 1947, after which it became known as Leith Citadel Goods Station. It closed on February 28 1968. Cars Nos. 172 and 148 meet as 172 prepares to reverse. This car was the penul-timate car to be built (in 1950) and was specially painted (see page 8) for the last week of tram working. *David Packer Collection.*

Below: The same scene on September 11 1989. The tower block in the background has changed the atmosphere dramatically, although many of the older buildings remain *in situ.* *Nigel Harris.*

Above: An instantly recognisable location at the foot of Leith Walk, with Standard car No. 219 about to depart for Colinton. To the right of the wartime Bedford lorry belonging to James T. Donald & Company is Leith Central station, built between 1898 and1903, and opened for passenger traffic on July 1 1903. Its traffic never matched its imposing facade and it closed on April 5 1952. It was converted as a Diesel Multiple Unit maintenance depot, but by the late 1970s it was disused. A range of proposals for its future was suggested, particularly a sports complex, but they came to nothing and the shed was demolished in 1988/89, leaving only the facade as a reminder of happier days. *LRT.*

Below: A splendidly animated shot of a police constable, apparently caught slapping a sergeant, at Salisbury Place! Shrubhill-built domed-roof Standard No. 164 leaves Newington Road, for Grange Road and Church Hill on Service 14. Much survives here in 1989: the Crawfords shop on the right is still in business, but 'Baird the Bootmaker' (who in 1946 had nine branches in the city) has now disappeared. The corner shop on the left is now Remnant Kings. Note the large 'Mortar and Pestle' over Boots the Chemist, on the left hand side; these apothecaries' symbols over shop windows can be seen in various locations in the city centre, even today. *LRT.*

Above: The centre traction poles stand out well in this view of Bernard Street, Leith, as Standard car No. 210 passes the Robert Burns statue, en route to Church Hill on Service No. 14. This statue was erected in 1898, but was subsequently removed from this location, to improve traffic flow. The domed building left of the tram was built as the Leith Bank in 1804-06. *LRT.*

Right: Hurst Nelson streamlined car No. 14 turns into Strathearn Place, on a quiet day in March 1954. This section of track was built to replace the horse-drawn route along Hope Terrace and Clinton Road. It was inspected and opened on June 1 1899 and the horse route had been lifted by February 1900. *LRT.*

Left: Church Hill, the terminus of the Granton Circle services Nos.13 and 14. Service 5 also passed here, but continued on to Morningside Station. The last cars ran from here in June 1956. An unidentified Standard car and domed-roof Standard No.164 pause before starting back for Granton. The relatively tranquil atmosphere remains much the same today. Note the dubious condition of the track on the right and the 'dropped' setts; these indications of neglect became an all-too-familiar feature in the tramway system's last days. *LRT.*

Right: There is something of a timeless quality at Marchmont, where the buildings remain much the same today, save for cleaning and repair. George Orr's Carpet Beating and Cleaning lorry retreats into the distance as Standard Car 233 prepares to turn into Beaufort Road on the circle service 6. The car carries an advert for the *Evening Dispatch*, which merged with the *Evening News* in 1963. The lettering on the litter bin on the left of the photograph reads: "In your hands rests the cleanliness of Edinburgh." These bins, set into the pavement, were a common feature of city life in the 1950s. *LRT.*

Above: The prototype of the latter-day steel-bodied cars, No. 180, stands in the spur at Merchiston Place, Bruntsfield on August 31 1955. This spur was used for short workings of Service 23, but was seldom in use latterly. This appears to be an enthusiasts special working. The surroundings have changed relatively little over the years. No. 180 entered service on Sunday April 3 1932 and was indeed a revolutionary vehicle, with many modern features, including an alloy frame with timber filling and metal panelling with straight sides, wider and deeper seats, air bells and tubular electric heaters, headlamp with dimmer, brake stop light and air operated windscreen wiper.It ran for three years in a striking livery of bright red earning it the nickname of 'Red Biddy; it survived virtually until the end of tram operation, in 1956. *R. Wiseman.*

Left : An unusually battered and work-stained Metro-Cammell streamlined car No. 29 passes by Holy Corner in 1954. The church on the right was the North Morningside Church of Scotland, designed by David Robertson in 1879-81 and which contains some fine stained glass. It is now used as a Community Centre, following the decision in 1979 of Morningside United Congregational Church to merge with North Morningside Church of Scotland. Morningside United Congregational Church, designed by James McLachlan in 1927-29 is on the site of the 1865 United Presbyterian Church by Robert Paterson and demolished in 1927. On the left is Christ Church, Morningside Episcopal Church of Scotland, designed by Hippolyte Jean Blane in 1875-78. H. J. Blane was a member of the Congregation and was the architect of many Edinburgh Buildings. *LRT.*

Left bottom: English Electric streamlined car No 20 pauses to pick up passengers in Bruntsfield Place, Boroughmuirhead. MaGavin Mavara Tea was a well known 'brew' in the 1950s and 1960s and was part of the McGavin and Sclanders tea merchants of 9 York Street, Glasgow. Crerars newsagents shop (still there in 1989) was advertising birthday cards, biro and citizen refills, platinum and scroll pens and shelf and crepe paper. Also on sale was the popular periodical of the time, *The Picture Post*, which on this occasion featured the" Jungle Murder of five missionaries. *David Packer.*

Above: A wet day in Musselburgh, in March 1954 ,with the Tollbooth on the left. Standard car No. 369 negotiates the interlaced track (constructed thus because of the narrowness of the street) on its way back to the other end of route 21, in Waterloo Place. As in several other photographs in these pages; a chemists shop appears. This view shows Boots on the left and Findlays further down on the right, beneath the Goodyear tyre advert. *LRT.*

Above: In September 1989, the Musselburgh Tollboth still dominates the scene, although many of the buildings on the right have been demolished in favour of providing a wider road. *N. Harris.*

Right: An SS Jaguar Coupe, an Austin Princess, an Austin A35 Saloon and an SMT/AEC Regal feature in this view as No. 65 crosses the bridge over the River Esk at Musselburgh on June 19 1954. The buildings on the right beyond the bridge have now been redeveloped. *R. Wiseman.*

Left, upper: A suburban scene at Fairmilehead terminus as car No. 41 reverses and prepares for the downhill run to Morningside station on its way to Granton Road station. The track to Fairmilehead from Braids was brought into use on April 19 1936, the penultimate extension to the system. The final extension was opened on St Valentines Day (February 14) 1937, when the last section of the Corstorphine route was introduced, to the Maybury. It was originally intended that the track shown here should be further extended to Hillend but this was never implemented. The traction poles and streetlights shown here survived until the 1970s. *LRT.*

Left: The narrow and often-congested thoroughfare of Duke Street, Leith, on a bright summers day in April 1954. Wooden-bodied Standard car No. 366 is about to rejoin the double track section before swinging left on the climb up Leith Walk, whilst working on Service 19, to Tollcross. The buildings on the immediate left are no longer there; they disappeared with the demolition of Leith Central station. *LRT.*

Below: The once-familiar scene of a tram rumbling over the Bernard Street swing bridge, Leith, on August 3 1953. Car No. 88, one of the last survivors and a participant in the final procession, makes the crossing on its way to Granton, on Service No. 17. This bridge was built in 1898-99 by Sir William Armstrong, to replace an earlier swing bridge which closed on May 24 1897. The bridge last opened to allow passage of a ship on September 12 1956 and was replaced by a non-opening concrete structure by 1963. *R. Wiseman.*

DEPOTS AND WORKS

Right: Works car No. 3 in Frederick Street at 3am one morning in March 1952. These cars, seldom seen during the daylight hours, carried workmen and their materials around the system after dark, during essential repairs and maintenance. They were usually cut-down and modified ex-service cars, rather than custom-built vehicles. *R. Gordon.*

Below: Edinburgh has always considered the cleanliness of its vehicles to be an important factor. An early form of automatic car wash is demonstrated here, using open-balcony Standard car 28 – water must have poured down the stairs like a waterfall! *LRT.*

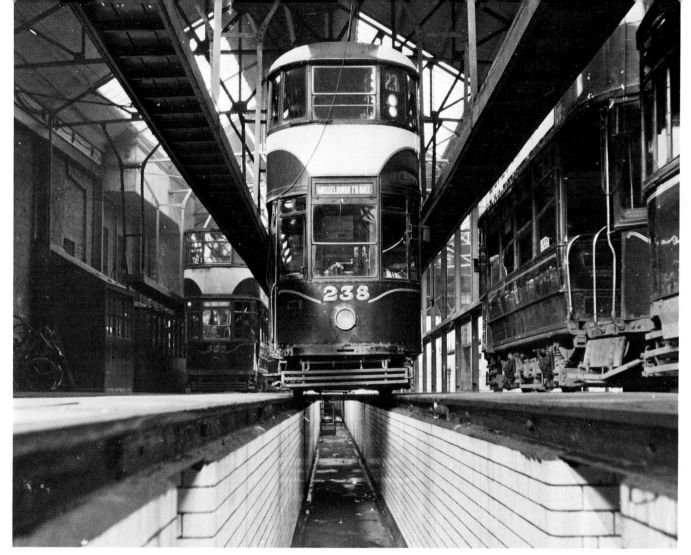

Above: A view from one of the car examination pits at Leith depot on April 11 1955. Modern flourescent lighting inside the pits was yet to be introduced, but nevertheless, the depot is clean and bright, to enable the brakefitters and other staff to carry out repairs. Car No. 357 (left, nearing withdrawal at this time) and 238 are amongst others awaiting their next turns of duty. Leith depot closed on May 5th 1956. *R. Wiseman.*

Left: Ex-Manchester 'Pilcher' car No. 196, which subsequently became No. 403 in its new home, en route for further service in Edinburgh. The city bought 11 of these cars between 1947-49, and all were delivered using similar Foden articulated lorries like this. The Pilcher cars were slightly longer than their Edinburgh counterparts and were normally confined to the comparatively straight routes from Waterloo Place to Portobello and Levanhall. All the Manchester cars were withdrawn after these services ceased in 1954. *LRT.*

Top: An official view of Car No. 261, one of the 'mongrels' produced at Shrubhill between 1932 and 1933. Although similar to the more familiar wooden-bodied Standard cars, there were subtle differences – noticeably the straight sides of the lower saloon – which enabled double seating to be fitted on both sides of the car. No. 261 was scrapped in 1955. *LRT.*

Above: A view of the upper and lower saloons of Hurst Nelson streamlined Car No. 11, built in 1935 and withdrawn in 1956. The lower saloon seats were generally upholstered in moquette, whilst the upper saloon seats were leather-covered. This arrangement did not apply in all cases, for many cars had leather seats in both saloons. At the time these photographs were taken, there was an 'Edinburgh Anti Fly Campaign' in full swing; the window adverts proclaim that 'one fly can breed 432,000 in seven weeks'. Dysentery and food poisoning were the after-effects of fly contamination and they should be looked on as 'wanted for murder — destroy!' *LRT.*

Left: A depressing scene at James Connell's yard, at Coatbridge, with Edinburgh cars being burned and scrapped. Each car was set ablaze to burn the wood and other unusable items, and the remains dismantled. A sad end to a familiar and much missed part of the Edinburgh scene. *Evening News.*

Below: A once-familiar scene which has changed considerably in recent years: Shrubhill workshops gates, with the parcels and lost property offices to the left and to the right. The chimney on the right is that which was attached to the cable power house; it still stands today. On the left is the chimney of the McDonald Road power station. *LRT.*

Right: Trams were transported to the scrapyard in this specially adapted vehicle. The condemned tram was driven under its own power between the shafts and was then jacked clear of the floor, and clamped in place. *LRT.*

Below: A most common sight in tramway days was the tower Wagon. Here we see an Austin vehicle, No 1 in the fleet, at the corner of Pilrig Street and Leith Walk with the two engineers aloft watching the world go by; car No. 216 approaches, the driver doubtless keeping a wary eye on the lady hurrying across the setts, seemingly oblivious to his presence. The driver has fitted a draught-excluding newspaper, jammed in the windscreen! Tower wagons were used for maintenance and repairs to the overhead electrical system. These vehicles were fitted with a radio telephone and could be quickly despatched to carry out emergency repairs. Although the Austin vehicle is now long gone, the actual wooden tower is still in service with Lothian Region Transport, now affixed to a Bedford lorry. *I. Blair.*

Right: The maintenance of a tramway system required some weird and wonderful machines! This is a portable electric grinder, used to give a smooth finish to the railhead after welding operations; electricity was provided by a generator lorry. Note that graffiti is not new, the wall in the background announcing to the world that: "Silcox is a fool" and "JS loves MV". *LRT.*

PRESERVED CARS

FROM a personal point of view, pride of place in this section of the book goes to car No. 35. Built at Shrubhill as a domed-roof Standard car, she first entered service in October1948 and was allocated to Leith Depot.

Only when this depot closed on May 5 1956 was No. 35 transferred to Tollcross, to see out the remaining days of her working life - or so it seemed.

In terms of tramway life, No. 35 was a comparative 'youngster' being only a mere 8 years old at the time of her withdrawal. As will be seen elsewhere in these pages, No. 35 was not originally scheduled for preservation, and would have met the same fate as the rest of the fleet at the hands of scrapmen at James Connell's yard, at Coatbridge. However, fate took a hand when sister cars Nos.189 and 225 collided at Morningside Station in September 1956. No. 225, earmarked for preservation, was too badly damaged and No. 35 was saved as 'the next best' car. She only carried three adverts during her working life: "Tide washes cleanest", "Dexter Weatherproofs – as British as the weather, but reliable" and "You'll feel much better if you drink more milk." The latter two are still on the car to this day.

No. 35's last noted day in service was on October 21 1956 from whence it was moved to Shrubhill. The car was stored here, following overhaul, until March 1961, when it was moved to nearby East London Street. Here, it received a full repaint and was displayed in this small museum building from July 1961 until 1963. Shrubhill works, in the meantime, had been modernised and plans for a larger museum were in hand. So, No. 35 was moved back to Shrubhill in September 1963 and the new museum was literally built round it, as shown on page 64.

It was intended that No. 35 should survive as a static exhibit, with never a thought to her ever running again – until a roof defect caused the museum to be closed in 1979. The Museum, which had been constructed 'around ' 35 was now demolished around her and she was even-

Above: Preserved car No. 35 passes the Playhouse cinema, in July 1955. The main feature showing at the time was "All for Mary' starring Kathleen Harrison, Nigel Patrick, David Tomlinson and Jill Day. Critics described the film thus: "A simple-minded farce in which two grown men with chicken pox, quail like children before a forceful old lady. On the strength of the latter characterisation and a few funny lines, the original play was a considerable success." The 'B' movie was entitled "Red' Sundown which starred, among others, Rory Calhoun. The Playhouse was built in 1927, with capacity for 3,048 patrons. It was designed as a dual purpose cinema and theatre; it suffered a lengthy closure before reopening after a major refurbishment in 1978-80. The advert on the side of No. 35 suggested that: "You'll feel much better if you drink more milk." The car is working on Service No. 19, from Craigentinny Avenue to Tollcross. *John Fozard.*

tually moved on March 21 1982 to Central Garage, Annandale Street. This movement was quite a novelty in itself. Although only a short distance, it was a delicate operation done under the cover of darkness. The car was lowered on to two ex-Atlantean bus axles and towed carefully by lorry to its new home.

Away from the public gaze, '35 was enshrouded in re-inforced polythene sheeting, to protect her, for the next 17 months. Its future was uncertain to say the least, then, for the second time in her life, fate stepped in again. This time, it was owing to the Blackpool Tramway Centenary, due to be celebrated in 1985. The story of 35's removal to Blackpool is long and complicated

and involved me in many hours of hard work, not to mention persuasive powers, to cajole the Department for National Savings (my employer) into 'sponsoring' the car for two years service in Blackpool.

To cut a long story short, it all happily came to pass and '35 left Edinburgh with due ceremony in November 1983, to travel to England via a circuitous route, to arrive in Blackpool on Saturday lunchtime, November 17 1983. The car was officially handed over to the safekeeping of Blackpool's transport department the following Monday, after being towed to North Pier for the formal handing-over ceremony.

Despite the local newspaper reporting that all that was needed was "a drop of oil and a few bits and pieces," much hard work had to be done to bring the car back to serviceable condition. It was a great personal thrill for me, having been involved so much in getting 35 to Blackpool, to be invited to travel on the car for the first time under her own power, for over 27 years, in January 1984. When she made her first public appearance in April 1984, '35 looked immaculate, following a partial repaint and a new coat of varnish.

Whilst in Blackpool the car ran without any major problems, save for a rather nasty collision near the end of her stay, and was popular with enthusiastic crews. They had great fun with the route colour lights and showing various Edinburgh destinations on the screens whilst in service up and down 'the Prom!' No. 35 stayed in Blackpool until transfer back to Scotland for service at the Glasgow Garden Festival in March 1988. Here she stayed for the duration of the Festival, carrying vast numbers of visitors, before removal to the National Tramway Museum at Crich in Derbyshire, in 1988. The car is to remain at Crich for the next four years by which time, perhaps, there will be somewhere in Scotland – maybe even Edinburgh – where she can run again. Meanwhile, if you are passing Crich, pop in and renew an acquaintance with an old friend!

There is, however, another Edinburgh tram which is 'preserved.' I use the term 'preserved' carefully, for the car concerned has survived for many years, not as a tram but as a holiday home in the Border country. Car No. 226 was originally an open-top cable car, built in 1903 by Dick Kerr and Company. It worked thus (with the addition of a top deck cover in 1907) until December 1923, when it was converted as an electric car, fitted with platform screens and a more

substantial top deck cover manufactured by McHardy & Elliott. Various seating alterations took place over the years and in June 1932 the top deck balcony was enclosed. In April 1938, the car was withdrawn and was sold for use as a holiday home at Hume. It remained there, until rescued by Lothian Region Transport in December 1987. It now rests in Central Garage and has been stripped and the decks separated, prior to rebuilding and restoration.

A great deal of hard work is now being undertaken, to restore the car to its final working condition. Who knows, one day Nos. 226 and 35 may

yet run again in their native city as a tourist attraction?

The lower deck of yet another car has lain at the bottom of a garden in Jordan Lane, Morningside for many years. Unfortunately, it had deteriorated over the years and was barely recognisable. However, the present owner gave permission for the removal of whatever useful bits and pieces could be salvaged, so car No.166 (built in 1899 as an open top cable car) converted to electric traction in 1923 and withdrawn in March 1931, is playing a part in the restoration of No. 226. We all look forward to seeing the restored car!